Three in a Tub

MARY JANE ZAKAS

Archway Publishing
1663 Liberty Drive
Bloomington, IN 47403
www.archwaypublishing.com
1 (888) 242-5904

ISBN: 978-1-4808-2054-8 (sc)
ISBN: 978-1-4808-2055-5 (hc)
ISBN: 978-1-4808-2056-2 (e)

Print information available on the last page.

Archway Publishing rev. date: 12/10/2015

Once upon a time

There was a nice lady who lived far from the city.
Isolated she's not, so there's no need to pity.

You see
No matter your where, or your time, or your space
No matter the weather, your likes, or your pace

You'll find
Folks at reading in their own time and place
Sharing a joy of the whole human race.

This lady, Roberta, likes tending garden with spade
Delighting in the beauty she has thoughtfully made.

But now on a journey she really must go
For winter is coming and so is the snow.

She'd put in her backpack the inflatable tub.
The one with neat wheels that come out with a rub.

She'd wear those cushioned shoes with springs you can't see.
The magazine said they'd be healthy for she.

They also had the built-in suction device.
She knew they'd be handy if walking on ice.

She'd wear pants with really cool pockets galore.
Hopefully, she wouldn't be needing one more!

She'd wear for a shirt her UV delight,
Avoiding sunburn: an unpleasant plight.

It had a thing in the threads of its weave.
So getting too hot was hard to conceive.

Finally, she'd pack some gloves and some lunches.
She knew they'd enjoy these nice little munches.

So, off she did set with one goal in her mind:
To bring home sweet apples, those one-of-a-kind,

To put on her table or can in a jar
For winter was only a little a-far.

Her jacket rolled up in its own little pocket
And swung from her waist like a missile or rocket.

Followed quite close by her cat and her dog,
She began her routine: a morning jog.

The cat liked following a short distance behind.
While the dog, staying close, was all set for a find.

but

A click of her tongue with a waving arm
And both of her pets would come like a charm.

At last

Almost there, her breath held tight;
Might those apples greet her sight?

Yes, alas, her trip not a waste.
Jump, thumbs up; so glad she'd made haste.

Some apples had fallen: a good sign from the tree.
Now ready for harvest they happened to be.

She strode toward the tree, her heart full of delight,
Happy that nature had brought forth such a sight.

Under the tree to her knees she did drop
Giving thanks for such a wonderful crop.

The dog and the cat knew what this was about
So into their places they hustled with clout.

16

The cat, Kitty Kay, on a branch she did tread.
She knocked down the apples with no bit of dread.

The dog, Gracie Jane, on the ground with great care,
Set apples by tub with her own little flair.

The lady, Roberta, with gloves on her hands
Was packing apples in tight circular bands.

They had almost packed the tub to its full
When black clouds came forth like a charging bull.

The rain began falling with a single splat,
But turned into a downpour in nothing flat.

Safe under the tree, the three tried not to worry.
We all know they hoped it would end in a hurry.

The minutes drug by --- forever--- each seemed
For now they must wait with their project gleaned.

Soon the lightening flashed bright, and the thunder rolled.
She thought, "What a beautiful thing to behold."

23

When the rain finally came to its end,
The sun crept out for a new weather trend.

24

Now homeward through grass and mud she was gliding,
For her shoes were made for this kind of striding.

Stopping, she noticed a fresh smell in the air,
She thought to herself, "That just *should not* be there."

She knew the next second it did *not* belong
For the smell in the air was ever so strong.

Then came a rumble, a noise that she knew.
A flash flood soon would be coming through.

The apples, she dumped right out of the tub.....
It just wouldn't do to die for some grub.

She hustled, loading the dog and the cat.
Soon safe in the tub all three of them sat.

The water arrived, just a trickle at first.
Then it seemed like a dam had suddenly burst.

Afloat they went with their eyes very wide.
She prayed no hole would be torn on their ride.

In the due course of time, the water receded
And on land they did put their feet unimpeded.

By now the sun was quite high in the sky
And she knew toward home they needed to fly.

They were far south now, so north they did head
Hoping their path would be easy to tred.

Hot-footing along, they happened to spy
Something not right with a cow and a guy.

Her calf, it seemed, had been frightened away
When the flood had haulted its pasture play.

Now, Roberta was glad to join in the search
For she lived what she had been taught in her church.

After an hour, maybe a bit more,
This caring group was still facing their chore.

Soon, Gracie Jane gave out one loud yelp.
She had found the calf in need of help.

34

Stuck in the mud, it found it a chore
To lift one leg, two legs, three legs, four.

One on each side, the man and Roberta got
With little luck tugging until they were hot.

Kitty Kay knew something had to be done;
Wallowing in mud is not any fun.

With kitty grace, she made a leap
Right on the calf's back - a sight to keep!

The calf in a dither and afraid for its life
Lurched upward as if lifted by God from its strife.

It lit on its feet and spinning around,
Heard its mother make a comforting sound.

It made no noise, just like wind in a ripple
And in a flash put its mouth 'round a nipple.

The man and Roberta sighed in relief,
The mother had now lost all of her grief.

The calf with its mom was a glorious sight,
Swelling their hearts as this bad start turned out right.

Roberta and the man laughed with glee
Now that there was no emergency.

At last she said they had to be going
For afternoon, the sun was now showing.

January 11, 2016

Rhonda Gould
812 North Steele Street
Tacoma, WA 98406

Greetings Ms. Chairman and Committee Members,

I was asked by Awards Coordinator, Courtney Jones, to write a cover letter to you explaining my special circumstances. My book, <u>Three in a Tub</u>, was in production over 8 months and became a live title on December 15. I received my hardback copies January 7, 2016.

<u>Three in a Tub</u> is a novella developing its plot in verse with a strong character that demonstrates good values. Each picture was painted freehand by California born artist, Roberta Owen. ALL were crafted with basic water colors specifically to illustrate the verse on its page.

I understand that I should leave our contact information. It is:

 Mary Jane Zakas   HC 72 Box 21406   Dyer, Nevada 89010   (702) 882-4481
mjwz99@hughes.net.

Roberta Owen   11991 Ritenour St.   Frazier Park CA. 93225   (661) 964-7887

Sincerely,

Mary Jane Zakas

Mary Jane Zakas

They trekked toward home feeling good:
Just the way you'd think they should.

The apples had floated and did not sink
So they were not as harmed as you might think.

Some along the way they found.
She didn't leave them on the ground.

Back to the tree they eventually got.
Roberta's new shoes were as good as she thought.

They picked more apples and packed them just right.
With a little luck, they'd be home before night.

Kitty Kay on the tub and Gracie beside -
Roberta now reviewed her day with some pride.

Adventure done, they arrived tired but cheery
To a relieved husband who had missed his dearie.

The night-light in the house gave a very soft glow
As together asleep the cat and dog did go.

So much had been said, but now there was no peep
For both nice people had drifted off to sleep.

Appendix A: Interesting Facts

1. The science of growing apples is called **Pomology** from Pomaceous meaning the plant has flowers.

2. Archeologists have evidence that apples have been around since 6,500 B.C.

3. Apples are thought to have originated in Central Asia.

4. The **Lady**, or **Api** apple is one of the oldest varieties in existence.

5. The only apple native to North America is the crabapple.

6. Apples are grown in all 50 states.

7. Apples are the second most valuable fruit grown in the U.S. (Oranges are first.)

8. There are over 8,000 varieties of apples grown worldwide, however, the United States grows about 2,500 of which 100 are great for marketing.

9. Apple trees need bees and other insects to pollinate their flowers to make fruit.

10. An average tree can yield about 400 apples or about 20 bushels. A bushel weighs 42 pounds.

11. It takes 4 or 5 years for most trees to start producing apples but they can live to be over 100.

12. For a tree to make each apple, it needs the energy from 50 leaves.

13. The apple skin holds most of the healthful benefits and should be eaten.

14. Each apple has 5 seed pockets or *carpels*. The average apple has 10 seeds, but the health of the tree and the type of apple affect that number.

15. Apples float because they are 25% air.

16. Apples help your bones stay strong, improve your memory, and lower cholesterol.

17. However we choose to eat them: in juice, cider, vinegar, applesauce, or dessert, we each eat about 65 apples per year.[1]

---

[1] Thanks to USDA National Agricultural Statistics Service/ United States Apple Association www.usapple.Org

Appendix A: Interesting Facts

1. Cats choose with whom they will bond.

2. They can recognize their owner's footprints hundreds of feet away.

3. People and cats have identical regions in their brains for emotions.

4. There are 40 recognized breeds of cats but The Egyptian Mau is probably the oldest.

5. The oldest pet cat was found in a 9,500 year-old grave on the Mediterranean island of Cyprus.

6. Cats and birds have a homing sense based on the angle of the sun, the earth's magnetic field, and their biological clock.

7. A mother cat gives birth in 58 to 65 days. She may have 1 to 9 kittens and can do so every 4 months. The largest litter on record was 19: 15 lived.

8. Cats can live for 20 years, but the oldest on record was 38.

9. Only domestic cats hold their tails vertical when walking. Wild cats hold their tails horizontally or between their legs.

10. While dogs can make about 10 different sounds, cats can make about 100!

11. Cats sleep about 2/3 of every day.

12. Female cats tend to be right pawed while male cats tend to be left pawed.

13. Cats knead when comfortable and relaxed.

14. Cat eyes can absorb more light than a human's so they see well at night.

15. The earliest ancestors to cats lived around 30 million years ago.

16. A cat's hearing is better than ours. They hear two octaves above us.

17. For a short distance, a cat can go 30 mph.

18. They can jump 5 times their own height.

19. Cats do not see color as well as humans.

**C
A
T**

20.   A balance organ in their inner ear and their eyes help them to land on their feet: the "righting effect"

21.   Cats only sweat through their footpads.

22.   Most cats do not have eyelashes, but do have a 3rd usually hidden eyelid that adds tears and cleans their eyes.

23.   Cats *can not* chew large chunks of food because they can't move their jaws sideways.

24.   Cats purr between 25 and 150 hertz.

25.   A cat's back has up to 53 loosely fitting vertebrae so it is extremely flexible. Humans have only 34.

26.   A cat can move each of its ears separately a full 180 degrees because they have 32 muscles. Humans have only 6.

27.   Since a cat does not have a collarbone, it can fit through any hole the size of its head.

28.   Do not feed cats : onions, garlic, green tomatoes, raw potatoes, chocolate, grapes, raisins, Tylenol or Aspirin as these can cause organ failure and death.

29.   Cats can detect an earthquake 10 or 15 minutes before we can because they are sensitive to vibrations.

30.   A cat takes 20 to 40 breaths per minute. Its normal pulse is 140 – 240 beats per minute.

31.   A cat is sick if its temperature drops below 100.5 degrees or is above 103 degrees.

32.   A cat's nose pad is ridged in its own unique pattern similar to human fingerprints. No two are the same.

33.   For their size, cats have the largest eyes of any mammal.[2]

---

[2] Thanks to randomhistory.com

Appendix A: Interesting Facts

1. A mother cow will walk miles to find her calf.

2. Cattle have one stomach, but it is divided into 4 chambers. They swallow and later re-chew their food until it is digested.

3. Cattle have such great panoramic vision they easily see predators coming.

4. Cattle can hear higher and lower frequencies than people.

5. Cattle form close friendships, and will babysit for one another.

6. Cows can live to be 20 years old.

7. Cows are generally milked twice a day: morning and evening.

8. A cow will give 5 or more gallons of milk daily depending upon its breed.

9. Dairies usually choose Holsteins for large milk production where a family farmer might choose a small Jersey (800 lb) because its milk has the highest percent of butterfat (5%).

10. Christopher Columbus brought cows to America on his second voyage.

11. Cows eat about 40 pounds of food and drink about a bathtub of water daily.

12. There are more than 800 breeds of cattle around the world.

13. Cows are plant eaters and are therefore herbivores.

14. Cows spend about 10 to 12 hours per day lying down.

15. A cow does not lap its water; it uses a sucking action.

16. A cow can produce an amazing 10 tons of manure per year.

17. It takes 10 quarts of milk to make 1 quart of cream. That quart of cream can be used to make either a pound of butter, or a quart and a half of ice cream.

18. A cow's udder has 4 sections to hold her milk.

19. The gestation period for a cow is the same as humans: 9 months.

20. Plastic milk jugs were introduced in 1967.

21. Louis Pasteur developed Pasteurizing milk in 1856.[3]

---

[3] Thanks to dairymoos.com

Appendix A: Interesting Facts

1. A dog's shoulder blades are unattached to the rest of the skeleton to allow it greater flexibility in running.

2. The shape of a dog's face suggests how long it will live. Dogs with sharp pointed faces generally live longer.

3. A puppy is born blind, deaf and toothless.

4. The Basenji is the world's only dog that does not bark.

5. A dog can locate the source of a sound in 1/600th of a second and can hear sounds 4 times farther away than a human can.

6. Touch is the first sense a dog develops. Their entire body, including paws is covered with touch sensitive nerve endings.

7. Like a cat, a dog's nose print is as unique as a human fingerprint and can be used to identify it.

8. Dogs see better when the light is dim.

9. Petting dogs is proven to lower blood pressure of dog owners.

10. The average dog can run about 19 miles per hour.

11. The oldest dog on record was an Australian cattle dog named Bluey, who lived 29 years and 5 months.

12. A person standing 300 yards away is almost invisible to a dog.

13. Dogs can smell a thousand times better than humans. We have 5 million smell-detecting cells while dogs have more than 220 million. The part of their brain that interprets smell is 4 times larger than in humans.

14. Dogs have about 1,700 taste buds, cats about 473, but humans have about 9,000.

15. A dog is about as smart as a three year old child. This means they can understand 150-200 words.[4]

---

[4] Thanks to randomhistory.com

Appendix A: Interesting Facts

1. Flash floods can happen in all 50 states.

2. Flash floods can bring walls of water 10 to 20 feet high.

3. A car can be swept away in as little as 2 feet of water, while you can fall in only 6 inches of moving water.

4. Flash floods can create quicksand. If you must walk through water do so where it is not moving and use a stick to check the firmness of the ground in front of you.

5. Anywhere it rains, there can be a flood.

6. There is a potential for flooding if: a) the soil is full of water, b) the ground is frozen and can't absorb it, or c) the ground is too dry to absorb it fast enough.

7. Flash floods occur within 6 hours after the rain that caused them.

8. Two important things to remember about flash floods are: the water rises rapidly as more and more streams join, and the water moves very fast at about 9 feet per second!

9. Flash floods carry debris and can move rocks weighing 100 pounds.

10. Water moving ten miles per hour is as powerful as wind gusts of 270 mph (434 kph). (2005 article in USA Today)

11. Avoid contact with any kind of floodwater as it may contain oil, gasoline, raw sewage or other harmful things.

12. Do not drink floodwater, and wash your hands thoroughly before eating.

13. The top 5 deadliest floods in the world occurred when the Huang He (Yellow) River in China exceeded its banks. As recently as 1931, thirty four thousand square miles of land was flooded leaving 80 million people homeless, and killing between 1 and 4 million people.[5]

---

[5] Thanks to livescience.com, and wickipedia.com

Appendix A: Interesting Facts

1. About 100 lightning strikes hit the earth every second.

2. Lightning can carry up to a billion volts of electricity.

3. The average lightning bolt releases enough energy to operate a 100-watt light bulb non-stop for 3 months.

4. Ball lightning is rare, and still puzzles scientists because it floats, glows, and bounces along not obeying the laws of gravity or physics.

5. Lightning is extremely hot. It can heat the air around it to temperatures five times hotter than the sun's surface.

6. The hot air around the flash causes the air to rapidly expand and vibrate creating thunder.

7. About 2,000 people are killed worldwide by lightning each year.

8. Those lucky enough to survive being hit by lightning may suffer memory loss, dizziness, weakness, and or numbness for the rest of their lives.

9. Lightning is the result of an imbalance between negative and positive charged particles.

10. The negative charge in the bottom of the cloud builds as rain, snow or ice particles bump each other. The force builds and pushes against the air seeking a path to connect to the closest positive charge of the earth.

11. The negative charge continues earthward at 136 mph until it is close enough to pull the earth's positive charge skyward.

12. As soon as these two opposite energies connect, they return up the path at about *62 million* miles per hour, which we see as lightning.[6]

---

[6] Thanks to kidsdiscover.com and environment.nationalgeographic.com

Appendix B: Stretch2Smart Level 1

Recall: Roberta left the house on her journey to get one-of-a-kind apples. What three items do we know were in her backpack?

Re-Arrange: Pick any page in the story. Put each word on its own piece of paper. Arrange these into three groups:

1. nouns (persons, places, or things)

2. verbs (words that show action, including the linking verbs is, are, was, were, am)

3. Those remaining.

Keep each pile separate, but be sure each word is visible. Begin by choosing a word from each pile. Then continue choosing whatever words you want to build your very own interesting sentence. The words not in your sentence are extra. Write down your sentence. Start over. Make another different sentence. Now you have 2 amazing sentences.

Re-Form-It: If there had been no apples on the tree, what might Roberta do as a *Plan B* to put apples on the table or can in a jar for winter? Explain why you are choosing this idea: what makes it logical or practical for her to do?

Realize: What is one important thing Roberta knew that helped her on the trip to be safe and get back home?

STRETCH2SMART

Recall: Roberta's husband was very relieved to have them back home.

What evidence is there (in the pictures or text) that she could, or could not have in some way communicated with him?

Re-Arrange: Pick something mentioned in the story, but not of major importance. What kind of background details or facts would you add to the story to give this event or thing more importance in the story?

Re-Form-It: If the calf had not leaped out of the mud, what would be your plan B to rescue it? Explain why your plan would work and what facts make it believable.

Realize: Roberta does not use a compass or satellite tracking (GPS), yet she knows which way to go to find the tree and her way home after the flood. What knowledge did she use to do that? Explain how that works.

Appendix B: Stretch2Smart Level 3

Recall: Roberta is familiar with flash floods. The first rule is to get to higher ground, which she could do because there is evidence that she is fit. She does not follow rule one! Why? Make your case to defend her actions using proof from the pictures, and from interesting facts about flash floods.

Re-Arrange: Let's start the story with the picture and stanza of the last page where they are fast asleep. What picture and its stanzas would be a good replacement as the last page. Why have you selected this to be the best way to close her adventure?

Re-Form-It: If the tub had tipped over or gotten a tear in it, what facts or probabilities would you put forth to support that she and the pets would get home with some apples as planned?

Realize: The story provides information that will help with your decision to determine three things that are part of Roberta's character (the real person that she is inside). Defend your reasoning with what happened in the story that made you aware of this character trait.

CPSIA information can be obtained
at www.ICGtesting.com
Printed in the USA
LVOW05*0025221215

467450LV00010B/35/P